ATTITUDE

TALK *it* UP

By Doris Gothard:

Seven Steps to Wealth

Finances & Spirituality

The Power of a New Attitude

Attitude: The Winner's Edge

To order, visit
www.dorisgothard.com
for information on other products.

YOUR ATTITUDES
ARE SHOWING

ATTITUDE IS THE SECRET TO *SUCCESS*

DORIS GOTHARD
FORWARD BY ELLEN MAYFIELD, PH.D, P.C.

To families, teachers, and leaders

from all over the world

who inspire others to have

a positive attitude.

AUTHOR'S PREFACE
A Word about This Book

The greatest discovery of my life is that a human being can alter life by altering attitude. What affects our lives most is not so much **WHAT** happens to us but more about **HOW** we react to what happens to us.

Our attitudes are …

- More important than facts.
- More important than education, money, circumstance, failures, successes, or what other people say or do.
- More important than appearance, giftedness, or skills.

We have a CHOICE in life every day regarding the attitude we will embrace for that day. Our successes and failures in life are caused more by our mental attitudes than by our mental capacities. It is possible to alter our attitudes and change our situations in life.

Attitudes reflect how we think and how we act towards other people. Don't let anyone tell you that your attitude is not important. Every day we show other people the thoughts we hold in our minds—through our attitudes. Here are some examples of the kind of thoughts we hold in our minds:

- "He or she has a poor attitude."
- "He must change his attitude or else."
- "Her attitude is positive."

- "His attitude is negative."
- "Her negative attitude towards her work assignment makes her uncooperative."
- "They don't associate with them because of their attitude."

Attitude is a choice. Attitude determines how we experience the world. If our attitudes are negative, we will have negative experiences.

Life is a matter of attitudes. There will always be the *positives* and *negatives* regarding people and things... goals and ambitions... right and wrong. The attitudes we choose every day will shape our lives every day.

Our attitudes form our future hopes in life; our perceptions of our peers, friends, and coworkers; and our successes and failures. Most people tend to wake up and accept ideas that reinforce their own attitudes!

Have you ever wondered why some people are more successful than others? There are links between our attitudes and what we accomplish in life. Don't allow little things to undermine your attitude. A positive attitude towards life and others will be the key to your success in life. There will always be conditions beyond your control – the weather, high prices, road conditions, the evening news, waiting in line, airline delays, losing something, having to work, the neighbors, relatives, etc. Regardless of your circumstance, CHOOSE to have a positive attitude.

The **key** to success in life is to have an "UP" spirit and a "CAN-DO" attitude. There are many people who succeed in life when others do not believe in them. But, rarely do people succeed when they **do not** believe in themselves. Practice positive self-talk every day!

If your attitudes include disbelief in yourself, fear, hesitancy, inner conflict, then life will give back to you disbelief, fear, hesitancy, and conflict.

But if you draw your attitudes from the power of your mind, life will give you the fulfillment of your dreams and ambitions.

Listen to YOURSELF as you talk to yourself about hopeful things. The way you think and talk about yourself today creates your tomorrows.

MIND YOUR ATTITUDE

A positive attitude is your best friend. A negative attitude is your worst enemy. Your greatest asset or your greatest liability is whether your attitude is positive or negative.

Your Attitudes Are Showing.
Shift your attitude into higher gear!

Doris Gothard

FORWARD

by Ellen Mayfield, Ph.D.
Certified School & Clinical Psychologist

"Change your perception, you change your attitude" is an old reframe that happens to be true. This of course is assuming one knows the definition of perception. *Perception* is a noun that is defined as one's ability to see, hear, or become aware of something through the use of our senses. Another way of looking at it is, the way we think about or understand someone or something, the ability to notice something easily.

Attitude is defined by many, including noted psychologists, as the way we think and feel about something or someone.

How are attitudes developed? Are we born with a natural disposition, or do we learn it? We as human beings are born with certain tendencies and through our relationships and experiences, much is developed.

Our parents or caregivers are our first teachers and/or role models. We learn how to interact with people by first interacting with our parents and watching them connect and relate to others. Our parents' reaction to a positive or negative situation is our first exposure to attitudes and how they affect our behavior and feelings. Children often imitate parents and learn by copying the way they speak, walk, and their intonations, hence, their attitude about situations and things.

As a psychologist, I encourage my clients to examine their attitudes regarding family, friends, and perhaps a relationship that is no longer working. Did their attitude change, and what may have been the reason or reasons for the change? Attitudes often change as we get older and have more experiences and interact with more people. Within our families, our parents rear their kids with a certain value system, structure, and expectation. When we look at our peers and their families that do not have the same value structure as our own, we stop to question why or why not. We are then gaining our very own perspective and attitude about something that is concrete.

As children, "fitting in" is of key importance to their acceptance. We see our children mimicking other children, and as parents we are quick to explain that the behavior is not something we wish for them to model. Our schools, churches, and our local communities are our proving grounds for teaching and modeling their learning and understanding of people. Positive and negative attitudes evolve from evaluating our personal experiences. More successes and failures from evaluating our personal experiences allow a broader perspective in our view about life, people, and values.

Who are our role models? How do they influence us? What standards do they set for us? In Social Psychology, attitudes are one major area of interest. Attitudes have a powerful effect on our behavior. Observational learning sets the tone for change. However, our behavior does not always represent our attitudes. Researchers suggest that people are more likely to behave in ways consistent with their attitudes when their beliefs are the result of direct experiences or when personally impacted by something or someone. Attitudes are measurable and changeable and influence our emotions and behavior.

Our diversity in the world has changed in the past 30 years. The way we see and interact with people cause us to alter our perceptions and views about them. One significant way in which this happens is through our travels. Travel allows us to see differences in people around the world and many times we see how our attitudes have been skewed by what we have heard and read.

Our activities allow individuals to see things from different perspectives, thereby allowing us to increase our positions and change others. This book will be an indispensable tool for young people, parents, and teachers to initiate discussions about change.

CHANGE YOUR PERCEPTION; CHANGE YOUR ATTITUDE.

Ellen Mayfield, Ph.D.
Clinical Psychologist, Private Practice
School Psychologist, Birmingham Public Schools
Instructor, Department of Clinical Psychology, Oakland Community College
Teaching Assistant, Department of Clinical Psychology, University of Detroit Mercy

Your ATTITUDE
is the key
to a better life.

TALK *it* **UP**
Everyday

THE JOURNEY BEGINS

As a child growing up in Alabama, nothing came easily for me. My grandfather (biracial) and my great grandfather (White landowner) were afforded more of life's privileges and comforts than I had simply because of the White color of their skin. Nurtured by my mother, grandparents, teachers, aunts, and uncles – I received an abundance of love from my family. They talked to me about the importance of a good education and a positive attitude regardless of my circumstances.

As soon as I was old enough to walk, my journey to unlock my potential began while picking cotton in the Alabama cotton fields. It was my first job. It's true! As a teenager, I picked and picked and picked cotton all day long, every day! It was hot! Oh my, it was hot! I could hardly breathe. I would look up and pray for rain so my work day could end. Picking cotton was an all day, sun-up to sun-down job.

Recently, on a hot Alabama summer day, I was reunited with the family for whom I picked cotton and cleaned homes, my first employer, the Cobb family. They said they always knew I would be successful in life because of my positive attitude and work ethic. They said they were proud of me and my success. My reunion with the Cobb family and my work experience in the Alabama cotton fields will be remembered with gratitude. The Cobb family is my family.

The experiences of my youth have taught me to have a positive attitude and a good work ethic, no matter what the circumstances. Working as a hired worker, picking cotton all day, and cleaning homes was my experience until I enrolled as a freshman in college.

My success story has had twists and turns. However, success is not a matter of luck. Success comes about as a result of being prepared. My choice to have a positive attitude about my personal circumstances in life helped to shape my future.

The cotton fields and a *positive attitude* prepared me to achieve a degree in Pure Mathematics with a minor in Engineering, receive a special invitation to attend President John F. Kennedy's White House Conference on Children & Youth, and have a successful career as a Corporate Manager in the automotive industry. For me, my life has been an incredible journey. A *positive attitude* is the **key** to a better life!

APPROACH EVERY JOB
as a
POSITIVE LEARNING EXPERIENCE

Success is not a
matter of luck.
Success comes about as
*a result of **being prepared.***

TALK it UP
everyday

ACT
"AS IF"
you are the
PERSON
YOU
WANT TO

BECOME

ATTITUDE=EVERYTHING

Good attitudes are demonstrated by being positive, encouraging, cooperative, etc. No one knows your thoughts, but most people can identify a person who has a good attitude. Here are some statements about someone who has a good attitude: "He or she is friendly and has a good attitude." "He or she has a positive attitude."

Virtually everyone remembers that one special person who earned the title of mentor or coach because of the help he/she gave you. Maybe it was a teacher, parent, grandparent, uncle, sister, or a neighbor. Maybe it was someone who appreciated your potential, gave you candid feedback, or forced you to be honest with yourself—someone who kept you on track and inspired you to go further than you ever thought possible.

Most people are
generally no smarter
than you.

TALK *it* **UP** *everyday*

BEFORE YOU CAN ACHIEVE THE TYPE OF LIFE YOU DESIRE

YOU MUST BECOME THE TYPE OF INDIVIDUAL YOU DESIRE TO BE.

Know WHO you are and WHAT you want to become in life. Begin to think, act, talk and conduct yourself as the person you want to be. Become the type of individual you desire to be by choosing a mentor or coach to help you achieve your goals in life.

If you believe you will succeed, you will succeed. Role play with the type of individual you want to become. You, and only you, are in charge of your goals in life. Think positively! A great attitude will propel you forward. Hard work, preparation, and a good attitude are the keys to success.

Remember, most people are generally no smarter than you!

BAD ATTITUDES

can be infectious.
Don't mimic the
bad attitudes of others.

TALK *it* **UP**
everyday

THE FUTURE HOLDS *great things* IN STORE FOR YOU.

PEERS

MAKE EVERY CONTACT WITH YOUR PEERS A POSITIVE LEARNING EXPERIENCE.

GOOD BEHAVIORS = GOOD RESULTS

There is an expression attributed to Dr. Ben Carson:

PEERS are persons, encouraging, errors, rudeness and stupidity. How others perceive you says a lot about your attitude. There is another expression which says "a picture is worth a thousand words." The following expressions tell a story and create a picture:

- "She is dressed inappropriately."

- "He is dressed inappropriately."

- "He has a poor attitude."

- "Her attitude is positive."

- "He has to change his attitude or else."

- "Her negative attitude towards her work assignment makes her uncooperative."

- "They do as they like because of their attitudes."

- "They don't associate with those people because of their attitude toward them as a group."

What people perceive **visually** is more powerful than what people hear you say **verbally**.

GOOD *attitudes*

=

GOOD *results.*

TALK *it* **UP** *everyday*

MOST PEOPLE CAN IDENTIFY PERSONS *who have* ... GOOD Attitudes.

Be a PERSON with a GOOD attitude and BELIEVE you will succeed.

A good attitude will help you learn something new, have a new experience, overcome fear, and find new friendships. A good attitude also helps define who you are and how you feel about things going on in your life.

Be a person with a good attitude by finishing high school with honors and academic scholarship awards. Get good advice. Believe you will succeed by graduating college and obtaining employment.

Good Attitudes = Good Results.

Since your mind can only hold ONE thought at a time, fill your mind with positive thoughts every day.

TALK *it* **UP** *everyday*

BE POSITIVE!
BE ENCOURAGING!

Everyone remembers that one special person who was ENCOURAGING.

Someone who kept you on track and INSPIRED you to go further than you ever thought possible.

BE A LEADER!

Make a decision to be positive! Be encouraging and don't allow anyone to cause you to react in any situation. Learn to be yourself and make your own decisions, regardless of what others think.

Listen to your gut. Hang with people who feel the same way you do. Learn to feel comfortable saying "no." Learn to make good choices.

Your attitude may seem trivial now, but it will be the key to your success later on in life. Make sure your friends are always encouraging you to display positive behaviors. Since your mind can only hold one thought at a time, fill your mind with positive thoughts. Be a leader!

People reflect back to you –
your ATTITUDE
towards them.

TALK *it* **UP**
everyday

Avoid

ERRORS

**A MISTAKE IS NOT A FAILURE.
HOW YOU HANDLE IT COULD BE.**

YOU ARE THE ONLY PERSON
WHO CAN AVOID NEGATIVE BEHAVIORS.

NO ONE ELSE CAN DO THAT FOR YOU.

ERRORS are caused by a lack of judgment. Something done wrong and left wrong is an ERROR – in need of correction. ERRORS can be as simple as a misspelled word. ERRORS and mistakes are not failures.

ERRORS can be an inappropriate reaction in a classroom when two students are fighting. Before you pick up a stick and try to break up the fight – call security. ERRORS can be an inappropriate reaction in a parking lot over a parking space. When sparks fly – keep your cool. Before things get out of hand – walk away from danger and trouble. A good rule – don't chase after trouble.

Avoid negative behaviors in associations with others. No one else can do that for you. Breaking the law, disruptive conduct at school or getting into trouble with your parents are examples of negative behaviors to avoid.

Avoid negative outward displays such as texting while driving, cheating on a test, or spending lots of money on yourself. Cheating and selfishness are bad behaviors and bad attitudes that should always be avoided.

Be the kind of person that others ENJOY being around.

TALK *it* **UP** *Everyday*

RUDENESS
will make others
miserable,
including you.

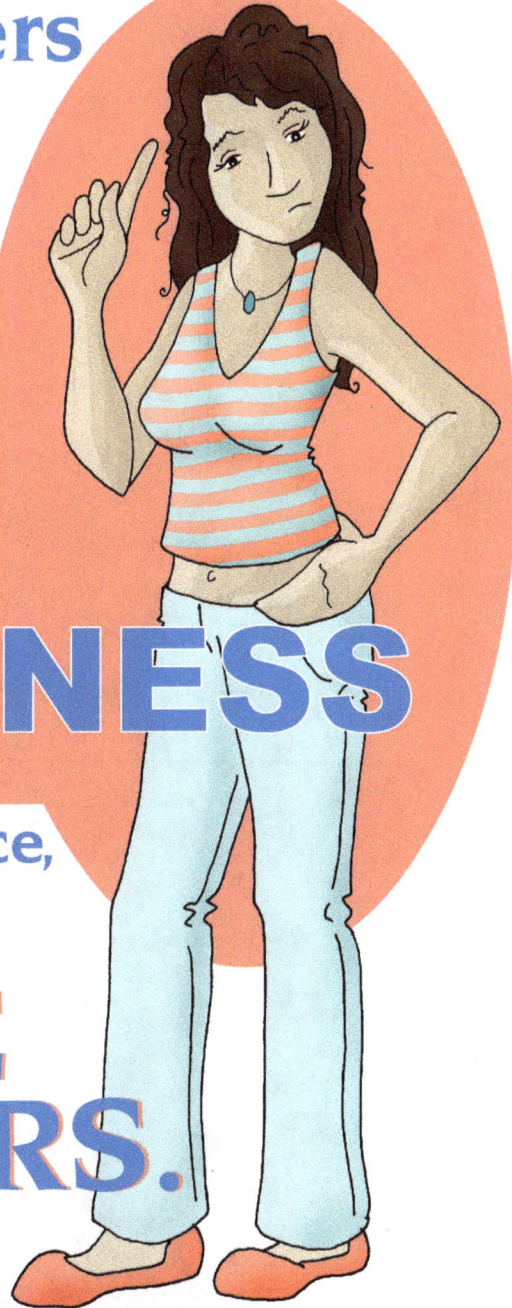

AVOID
RUDENESS

In every circumstance,
CHOOSE
POSITIVE
BEHAVIORS.

Offensive behaviors can be disruptive. Are you the kind of person others ENJOY being around? Do you act in a deliberate way to draw attention to yourself by being discourteous and impolite?

Learn to be respectful in your personal behaviors. You don't have to show people WHO you are in a negative way. Rudeness will always make others miserable, including you.

RUDE attitudes, manners, and behaviors offend, and persons who are RUDE generally don't care about other people. Be responsible. Choose positive behaviors!

When a less-informed person tries to give you a hard time – don't react as he would. Smile it off. Rise above it!

TALK *it* **UP** *everyday*

STUPIDITY
GET OUT OF YOUR OWN WAY

BE SMART.

"The definition of STUPIDITY is doing the same thing over and over again and expecting different results."
Albert Einstein

Look on the brighter side. Mistakes will happen. However, most mistakes can be corrected. Learn to associate with people who have the same high standards as you do. Learn to develop friendships with people who will help keep you on the right course. The most cherished reward is that of a mentor's hard-earned approval that you made the right decision to change your attitude and change your future. *Be smart!*

Most people don't think about their attitudes. Most people wake up and react to whatever happens to them. Think!

TALK *it* **UP** *everyday*

It is your ATTITUDE toward life that will determine Life's ATTITUDE toward you.

CHECK the MIRROR.

Look in the mirror! It's time to take charge!

Your attitude is a reflection of the person inside. You have the power to choose your attitude. Keep your mind on things that are good. If you dwell on negative things, your attitude will reflect negative things, and you will be whipped before you start your day. Look in the mirror. Part of the right attitude is to have a "winning attitude."

Accept yourself! Choose to have a positive attitude no matter what you decide to do in life.

Our attitude, opinions, and thoughts do matter! Only our own thoughts, words, and attitudes can hurt us. The path to a successful attitude is NOT as difficult as we might think. Each time we overcome an obstacle, our path to success becomes easier. Our attitude will, to a large degree, determine the eventual results in our life.

Say out **LOUD** to yourself: My new attitude is one of life's privileges. MY success in life will come as a result of MY being prepared. MY success in life will not be a matter of luck but hard work, preparation, and a positive attitude. It will take hard work to be successful. But— MY rewards in life will be the results of MY efforts. The way I talk about MYSELF today, creates MY tomorrow. MY good attitude is a continuous journey. MY good attitude will help me through tough times.

Everything we do must be done with and through other people. What affects them most is your ATTITUDE.

TALK *it* **UP** *everyday*

CHECK YOUR ATTITUDE! The problem is not the problem. The problem is your ATTITUDE toward the problem. Choose YOUR attitude every day.

CHECK YOURSELF. Ask yourself this question: Am I killing myself with my own attitude?

A positive attitude will take you to places you have always dreamed of. Don't let things you cannot control undermine your choice of a positive attitude.

Some of the most important **attitude traits** for a good leader are excellent work ethic, a pleasing personality, and the skill of **listening**.

TALK *it* **UP** *Everyday*

THE DEEPEST CRAVING
OF EVERY HUMAN BEING
IS TO FEEL
APPRECIATED.

ENCOURAGE
ENABLE
EMPOWER!
BECOME A MENTOR

Treat every contact with another person as a learning experience. There are links between the CHOICES we make and what we accomplish. Get excited about opportunities to CHOOSE. The future holds great things in store for you when you make right choices in life. Make a decision to change, learn, and improve the choices you make in life. Remember: You can choose your attitude.

When someone does something kind for you, recognize it. **Say, "Thank you."** Make others feel needed, important, and appreciated, and they will return the same to you. A simple "thank you" goes a long way.

Everyone likes to feel that they are of value and that they count. Encouraging words are essential to life. Just as a plant needs water, we all need a little encouragement from time to time. We all make mistakes. We all need encouragement to help us evaluate our mistakes. An attitude of gratitude is important because attitude truly is everything! It drives virtually every decision you make and how you live each day of your life. Attitude either propels you forward or holds you back. While the external circumstances in your life can be chaotic, your attitude is the key to a better life. Are you in need of encouragement? You are not alone. Be confident. Know what you want in life.

Expect to reach the goals
you set for yourself.
Expect the best and get it!

TALK *it* **UP**
everyday

Eli Whitney had an OPTIMISTIC attitude. Eli Whitney's invention of the cotton gin revolutionized the cotton industry in the United States. Prior to his invention, farming cotton required hundreds of man hours to separate the cottonseed from the raw cotton fibers. Many people said his machine would put thousands of people out of work. Instead, the invention made the production of cloth much cheaper, and millions of people were able to buy more clothing, which created countless jobs.

Charles Babbage had an OPTIMISTIC attitude. Charles Babbage Is best known as "the father of the computer." It is believed that Charles Babbage invented the concept of a programmable computer because he did not like doing his own calculations by hand. When he invented the programmable computer, many people believed they would lose their jobs to technology. Almost everyone will agree that computers have improved how we communicate.

Part of the right mental attitude is to look for the best in new ideas. Be optimistic. You can become an inventor or start your own business. You too can dream the impossible!

Maggie Lee Sayre had an OPTIMISTIC attitude. Maggie Lee Sayre was born deaf near Paducah, Kentucky, in 1920. She lived 51 years of her life on a river houseboat as her family made a living fishing throughout Kentucky and Tennessee. During her life she did not see her deafness as a handicap but an opportunity to unlock her potential. She used her camera to take black and white pictures that changed the way we view our world.

Madam C.J. Walker had an OPTIMISTIC attitude. Madam Walker, the first female millionaire, was born to slave parents who were sharecroppers in Delta, Louisiana. Her journey began in the cotton fields of the South. The people she worked for promoted her from the cotton fields to work as a washerwoman, and from washerwoman she was promoted to kitchen cook. Later in life she bought her own land, built her own factory, and promoted herself into the business of manufacturing hair products.

Harriet Tubman had an OPTIMISTIC attitude. Born in Maryland into slavery as a child, she was one of 11 children. She was beaten by the master for whom she was hired to work. At an early age she suffered a head wound when hit by a heavy metal weight, which caused disabling health problems throughout her life. As a runaway slave, she fled for her life to Philadelphia to escape slavery in Maryland. Not satisfied with her own freedom, she returned immediately to Maryland to deliver hundreds of other slaves to freedom with the help of a network of activists and safe houses known as the Underground Railroad.

In spite of her numerous health challenges (severe headaches, dizziness, dreams, etc.), Harriet Tubman (also known as "Moses") was a courageous fighter for women's suffrage and Civil Rights. Because of her poor health, it was no easy task for her to mobilize slaves to freedom, but with a positive attitude and determination, she was prepared to lead her people out of slavery.

Choose to have an OPTIMISTIC attitude. It will pave the way for you to unlock your potential! Change your attitude! Change your world!

You are of value
and worth.

TALK it UP
everyday

STAMP YOUR OWN VALUE UPON YOURSELF

IT DOESN'T MATTER WHAT YOU DO IN LIFE UNTIL YOU ACCEPT YOUR OWN WORTH.

TOTAL ACCEPTANCE–A PRICELESS GIFT!

Anything can be accomplished with the right attitude. Expand the boundaries of your thinking. Tell yourself that you are of value and worth. Set high standards for yourself. If you believe you are going to succeed, you will succeed! Anything can be accomplished if you have a positive attitude and believe in yourself. Nothing beats having a good attitude. Once you accept your own worth, your value is *priceless!*

Your attitude is a reflection of the person inside.

TALK *it* **UP** *everyday*

YOU can SHAPE your life by your ATTITUDE.

MAKE QUIET TIME A PART OF YOUR DAILY LIFE.

THINK POSITIVELY

ACT POSITIVELY

Your attitude is a reflection of the person inside. Make quiet time a part of your day to help you build a positive "can-do" attitude such as humility, curiosity, empathy, and trust. The most powerful force is what you think. Only our own thoughts, words, and attitudes can hurt us.

When faced with a challenge in life, try to discipline yourself to think positively. Positive things happen to positive people. When your attitude is positive, you will master your difficulties.

Remember: Choose your attitude—choose your power! DON'T let life's challenges get you down!

When you find yourself in a difficult situation, DON'T despair. Your head is your greatest asset. The chief purpose of your body is to carry your brain around. It is your mind, working in a calm, cool fashion that solves your problems. Failure is not the last word! Keep your thoughts under disciplined control—no drugs, no alcohol, no tobacco. Cultivate the right attitude that will help you succeed in the end.

Choose to see your setbacks as doorways to opportunities and adventures instead of adversities, confinements, challenges, and dungeons. When you welcome your problem without resentment, you can cut its size in half. You can be shaped and molded by your problems, or you can be challenged and motivated by them.

The right attitude at the beginning of your day will affect the outcome more than anything else. Say, "Yes, I can! Yes, I will change my attitude!" You are IN CHARGE. What you say, think, and do builds confidence! A negative attitude will never defeat a person who thinks and acts positively.

Expect to succeed more often than you expect to fail.

TALK *it* **UP** *everyday*

The KEY to success in life is to have a CAN-DO attitude.

TALK *it* UP

When someone does something kind to help you overcome and succeed say "Thank You."

Your attitude is intertwined with the roles you play in life…how you see yourself in life, how you really are, and how others see the attitudes you show. When you have a positive attitude, good health, family, and good friends, little else is needed to be successful in life.

Make a decision to find someone who can help you overcome and succeed. Have an attitude that says, "I am going to learn something new today."

Remember: When someone does something kind to help you succeed, say, "Thank you!" Your attitude, more than anything else, will determine your success or failure. Your CAN-DO *attitude* will determine your *altitude* in life.

Your attitude is something
that can be <u>controlled</u>
and <u>changed</u>.

TALK *it* **UP**
everyday

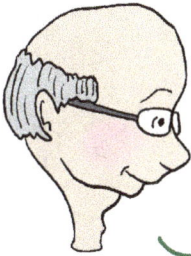

Avoid talking about serious personal problems with anyone who can't solve them. Use the power of your CHOICE to do "self-talk."

Learn to choose positive relationships with people who yearn to learn. Learn to make your own decisions, regardless of what another person is encouraging you to do. Learn to demonstrate positive attitudes and a manner of conducting yourself positively at all times. Choose people you can learn more from and who are positive role models.

Do self-talk! Your attitude is something that can be changed and controlled.

*Choose to have a positive
attitude every day.*

TALK *it* **UP**
Everyday

At the beginning of every day, make a decision to offer friendship, encouragement, and guidance to another person. You don't need special skills, just the ability to care and listen.

With a positive attitude, you can brighten someone else's day. If you think you're having a bad day, just add a quart of positive attitude and enjoy the rest of your day. Occasionally our cars run low on motor oil, and we have to add a quart. Make a decision to be positive every day.

When you CHANGE the
way you see things –
the things you see will
CHANGE.

TALK *it* **UP**
everyday

Nothing can stop a person with the right attitude from achieving his or her goal; nothing on earth can help a person with the wrong attitude. Don't allow anyone to ruin your day by raining on your parade! When some less informed person has tried to ruin your day by giving you a hard time, don't react as he or she would. Don't mimic the bad attitudes of others. Overcome negativity by thinking positively! Just smile it off! Rise above it!

FEAR of failure does influence our attitude. If you have the fear of failure, honestly face the possibility that your attitude may be the cause. Take responsibility. Be honest. If you are afraid to face up honestly about your attitude in life, you may be afraid to see YOU as you really are. KNOW who you really are. Accept yourself! Believe in yourself! It is the only way to get rid of fear.

Feed your attitude with good thoughts daily. Learn to develop good attitudes by dwelling on things that are good. If you dwell on negative thoughts, your attitude will reflect negative thoughts. Your attitude in life will determine your success in life. The key is to act as the person you want to become. Ask yourself the following questions:

- Do I always do my best?
- Am I friendly and cooperative?
- Do I attend to details?
- Am I optimistic?
- Do I do more than my share?
- Am I well-mannered?
- Do I follow through?
- Am I believable?

*Radiate an attitude of
well-being and confidence.*

TALKit**UP**
everyday

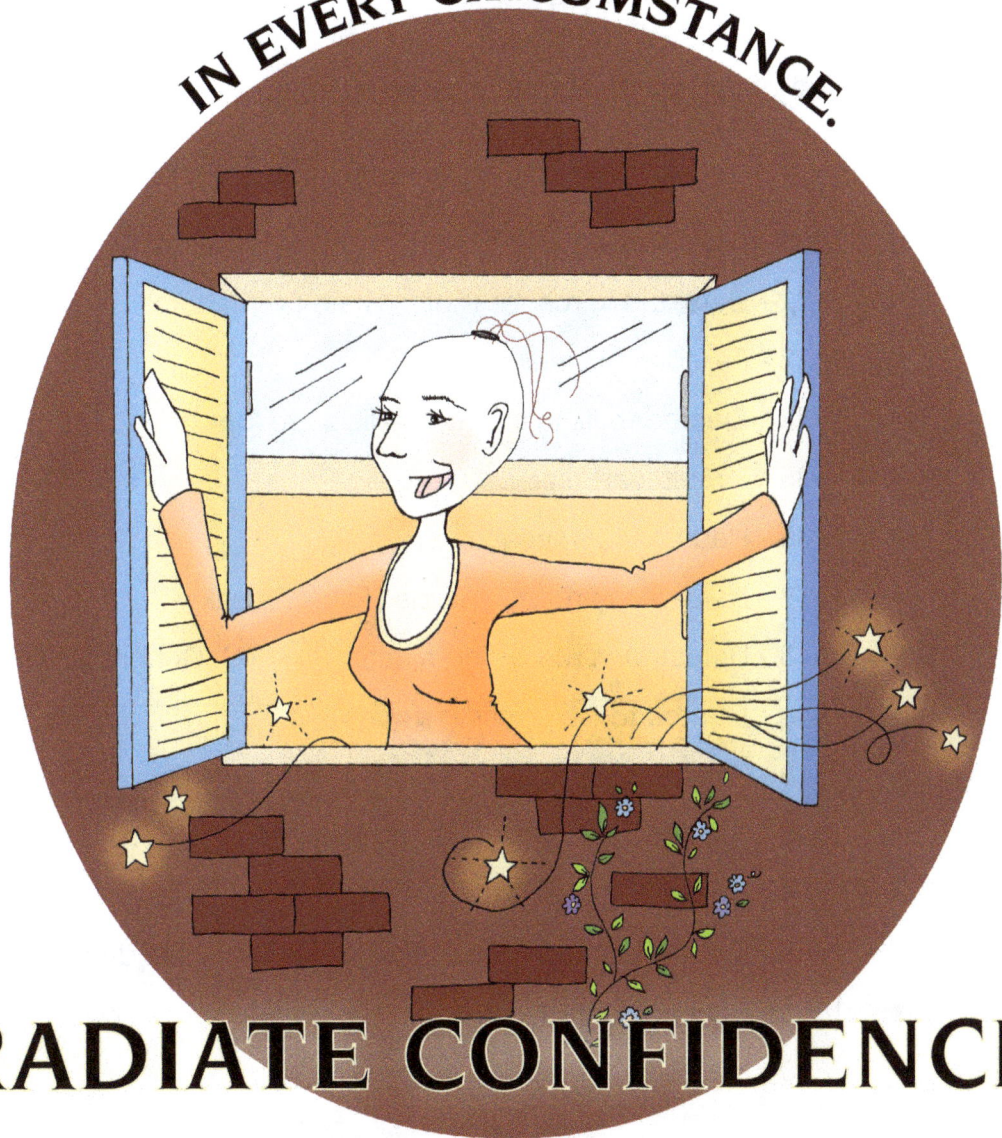

Abraham Lincoln rose from humble beginnings. He had less than a year of formal education prior to running for political office. Before becoming President of the United States, Abraham Lincoln endured a steady stream of failure and defeat. He was born into poverty. He could have quit, but he didn't. He never gave up!

Here is a list of failures of Abraham Lincoln (along with a few successes)[1]:

- 1831 - Lost his job
- 1832 - Defeated in run for Illinois State Legislature
- 1833 - Failed in business
- 1834 - Elected to Illinois State Legislature (**success**)
- 1835 - Sweetheart died
- 1836 - Had nervous breakdown
- 1838 - Defeated in run for Illinois House Speaker
- 1843 - Defeated in run for nomination for U.S. Congress
- 1846 - Elected to Congress (**success**)
- 1848 - Lost re-nomination
- 1849 - Rejected for land officer position
- 1854 - Defeated in run for U.S. Senate
- 1856 - Defeated in run for nomination for Vice President
- 1858 - Again defeated in run for U.S. Senate
- 1860 - Elected President (**success**)

---

1 Kurtus, Ron. "Failures of Abraham Lincoln." School for Champions. 11 January 2007. Web. 14 May 2011. <http://www.school-for-champions.com/history/lincoln_failures.htm>.

Abraham Lincoln's résumé looks pretty glum, making you wonder how he ever made it to the top. But when you think about it, in order to run for office or high positions so many times, you have to have something on the ball and have more successes than meet the eye.

Abraham Lincoln is an excellent example of the *power of a new attitude.* He never quit trying, and his positive attitude for success was key to his election as the 16th President of the United States.

Thomas Edison failed thousands of times while attempting to invent the light bulb. He is reported to have said that the attempts were not failures but opportunities to know how <u>not</u> to create a light bulb. Shortly thereafter, Edison invented the light bulb. A mistake is not a failure.

*A positive attitude is the
key to success in life.*

TALK *it* **UP**
everyday

CHANGE YOUR PERSPECTIVE

I CAN'T	I CAN
I WON'T	I WILL
I DOUBT	I AM SURE
I FEAR THAT	I AM CONFIDENT THAT
I'LL WAIT & SEE WHAT HAPPENS	I'LL MAKE IT HAPPEN
IT'S NO USE, I'M BEAT	I CANNOT BE BEATEN
IT WON'T WORK	IT WILL WORK
I DON'T HAVE TIME	I'LL MAKE TIME
I'M TOO OLD (OR TOO YOUNG)	MY AGE WON'T STOP ME
I DON'T HAVE THE SKILLS	I'LL DEVELOP THE SKILLS

Lou Holtz, one of college football's most successful coaches, said it best when he said, "Ability is what you're capable of doing. Motivation determines what you do. Attitude determines how well you do it."[2]

The most important years of your life are the school years to prepare you for the many years remaining in your life after school. How well you do in your school years depends upon your attitude towards your school work.

The Stages of Life is something young people who are still in school should think about. Regardless of your age, if you are in school, think about the stages of your life. Let's assume you will work until you are 66 years old before you retire. This 40-year span takes up 47% of your life. When you retire, you will have a life of 20 years left, or 22% of your total lifespan. All together you will have a period of 60 years, or 69% of your life, remaining after educating yourself for your work and retirement years. If you do not go on to college after high school, you will have to add another eight years to your working life. Consider the kind of life you'll have if you do not prepare yourself for a working life that you should want to enjoy.

Consider what the 20 years in retirement will be like if you have not prepared yourself for retirement. If you only have Social Security to provide you with income in your retirement years, you'll be living at the poverty level. It will be even worse than that if Social Security is not available to you in the future.

---

2 http://www.goodreads.com/author/quotes/85179.Lou_Holtz

What kind of life do you want to have for the majority years of your life – your retirement years? A lot will depend on your attitude during your school preparation years. It's up to you to make the right decisions throughout your lifetime. Your school years are the most important years to prepare for the rest of your life. This book is an attempt to provide the guidelines needed to develop an attitude for success throughout your life.

The attitudes you SHOW
to others, create your future.

TALK *it* **UP** *everyday*

Your Attitudes Are Showing was an idea inspired by the life and work of Dr. G. Herbert "Herb" True. The ways in which we live and respond are the keys to developing a positive attitude. I would consider myself to have failed had it not been for the mentoring I received from my family about my attitude and my actions. Everything they said and did was centered on helping me to be the best I could be in life.

Like most people, I have felt misunderstood and in need of someone to help me refocus on my goals. My attitude today reflects tremendous love and respect to my family, teachers and friends for helping shape my life. Attitude <u>is</u> the key to success. The positive attitudes you SHOW to others will create your success in life.

People want to feel
recognized and needed –
to know that they count.
When they feel these things,
they will succeed.

TALK *it* **UP**
everyday

THE ATTITUDE
GOLDEN RULE

FOR THE NEXT 30 DAYS TREAT EVERYONE AS THE MOST IMPORTANT PERSON ON EARTH

Most people want to feel recognized, appreciated, and needed. Most people want to feel that they count. When they feel these things, they will give you their love and respect, and they will buy whatever products you sell. For the next thirty days, treat others the way they want to be treated, and they will return the favor.

Most people don't think that their attitudes matter. They wake up and react to whatever happens to them. Don't react. Your attitude is something that can be controlled. Your attitude determines who is rider and who is horse. You have a choice. You either ride life, or it rides you. The secret to the success in your life is whether your attitude is positive or negative!

Choose to have a positive attitude and make a difference in the world. Always be positive. Think success, not failure. Nothing can stop the person with the right mental attitude from achieving his or her goal; nothing on earth can help the person with the wrong mental attitude. Say to yourself: "The problem is not the problem. The problem is my attitude about the problem."

In life, success or failure is determined more by our attitude than by our mental capacities. It pays to build an attitude of confidence every day. It pays to believe in yourself every day! The most powerful force you have is what you say to yourself and believe.

Remember—**Your Attitudes Are Showing!** *For the next 30 days –* treat everyone as the most important person on earth!

MIND YOUR ATTITUDE

MIND YOUR ATTITUDE is an expression that says: Attitude is important. Pay attention to your attitude every day! Stop telling yourself that your attitude is not important.

MIND YOUR ATTITUDE says: Caution, be careful, watch, keep calm, and think before you speak.

Attitude is important. We MIND that you may miss out on a successful life. MIND YOUR ATTITUDE every day.

Doris Gothard

FROM A CHILD OF THE ALABAMA COTTON FIELDS TO CHILDREN ALL OVER THE WORLD ...

The story in this book about the importance of a positive **attitude** is based on my own childhood recollections of growing up in Alabama. I was amazed and excited when I realized I could write simple narratives with illustrations, and they could be transformed into a book about **attitude** for children all over the world.

Most children around the world spend 5 years or 6% of their life at home before going to school. They spend 9 years or 10% of their life in kindergarten through eighth grade.

Most children around the world spend 4 years or 5% of their life in ninth grade to twelfth grade. When they graduate from high school and go on to a college or university, they may spend 4 years or 5% of their life preparing themselves for a college career.

When college graduates go on to graduate school to get an advanced degree, they may spend another 5 years in graduate school for an advanced degree. Preparation in school can take up to 26 years of a student's total life.

When students are finished with their schooling, they begin their working life stage for another 40- to 50-year span. It is important for every young person to consider what kind of life they will have if they do not prepare themselves for their working life.

What kind of life do you want to have during your retirement years? You must consider what 20-30 years in retirement will be like if you have not prepared yourself. Social Security may not be available in the future.

This book is an attempt to provide the inspiration needed for the school years of ages 7 and up, all over the world, to develop an **attitude for success.** In the end, it will be up to each individual to make the right decisions throughout their lifetime.

– Doris Gothard

TO FAMILIES AND TEACHERS

In a recent meeting which I attended, there were many high school students present. When asked what in their life needed to be improved, the majority of them responded: **"My attitude."**

Worldwide, there are conversations and discussions by focus groups about the challenges facing young people. Teens are faced with communication issues with parents, spiritual issues, fear of being homeless, addictions, prison time, and attitude problems.

We must help solve the issues of relationships, sex, love, health, identity, etc. facing teens. They are showing their troubled attitudes about life through drive-by shootings and violent attacks with knives and guns in schools. There are far too many children in the world who are victims of teen violence, gangs, bullying, abuse, and drugs.

As members of our communities, we have an obligation to help others. The least we can do is talk to young people about the importance of having a positive attitude in life.

Families and teachers realize that most students no longer work in cotton fields. Today, students have many more choices. One of the most important choices in a student's life is choosing a field of study – business, law, engineering, manufacturing, education, health, etc.

Because there are so many choices, we have an opportunity to have discussions with young people about the importance of a positive attitude to determine what they might want to do when they grow up or share ideas about what the author of this book did with her life.

Students must be encouraged to make choices with the optimistic belief that they will succeed in life. Advice from parents, teachers and counselors will have an impact on their decision-making process, but the greater impact on their choice for a successful life is personal preferences and interests.

Attitude is the key to a better life. Younger readers should understand that my story may not be their story. Through conversations using this book, **Your Attitudes Are Showing,** I hope that anyone who reads the book will begin to think about their attitudes and the need to make the kind of choices which lead to success in life.

– Doris Gothard

ATTITUDE

TALK *it* UP